Power Maths

Year 1
Practice Book 1C

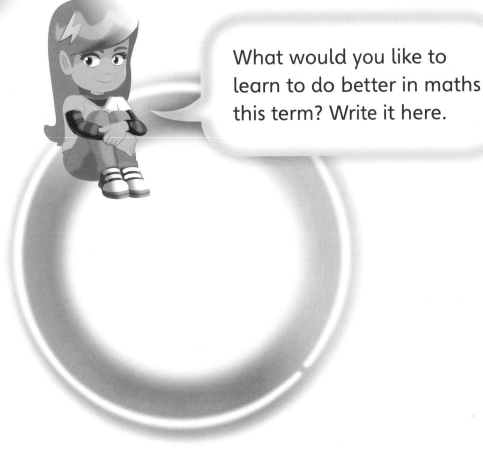

What would you like to learn to do better in maths this term? Write it here.

White Rose Maths Edition

This book belongs to _____ .

My class is _____ .

Series editor: Tony Staneff

Lead author: Josh Lury

Consultant (first edition): Professor Liu Jian and Professor Zhang Dan

Author team (first edition): Tony Staneff, Josh Lury, Kelsey Brown, Jenny Lewis, Beth Smith, Paul Wrangles, Liu Jian, Zhou Da, Zhang Dan, Yan Lili and Wang Mingming

Contents

I can't wait to have a go at these things!

It's time for the next part of our maths journey!

How to use this book

Do you remember how to use this Practice Book?

Use the Textbook first to learn how to solve this type of problem.

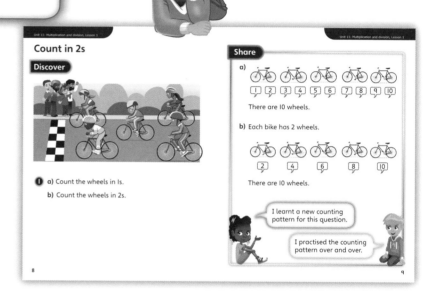

This shows you which Textbook page to use.

Have a go at questions by yourself using this Practice Book. Use what you have learnt.

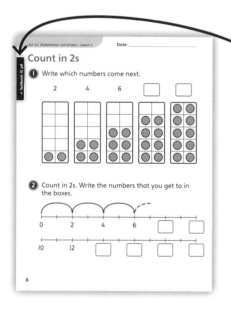

Challenge questions make you think hard!

Questions with this light bulb make you think differently.

Reflect

Each lesson ends with a Reflect question so you can show how much you have learnt.

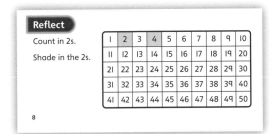

Show what you have done in My Power Points at the back of this book.

My journal

At the end of a unit your teacher will ask you to fill in My journal.

This will help you show how much you can do now that you have finished the unit.

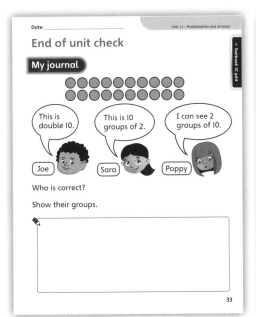

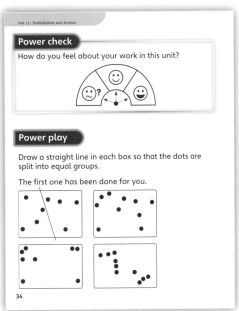

Date: _____

Count in 2s

1 Write which numbers come next.

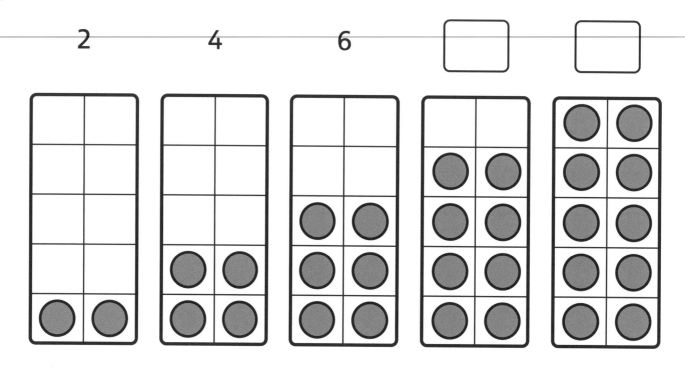

2   4   6

2 Count in 2s. Write the numbers that you get to in the boxes.

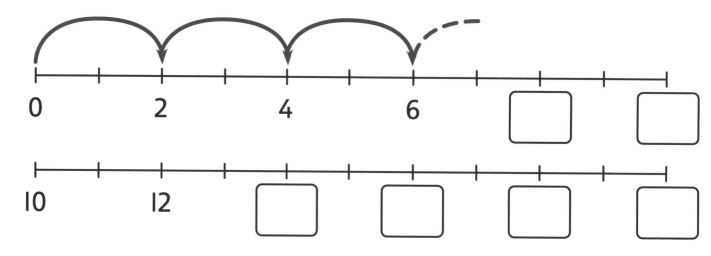

0   2   4   6

10   12

6

3 Count in 2s. Write the number of 2s in the box.

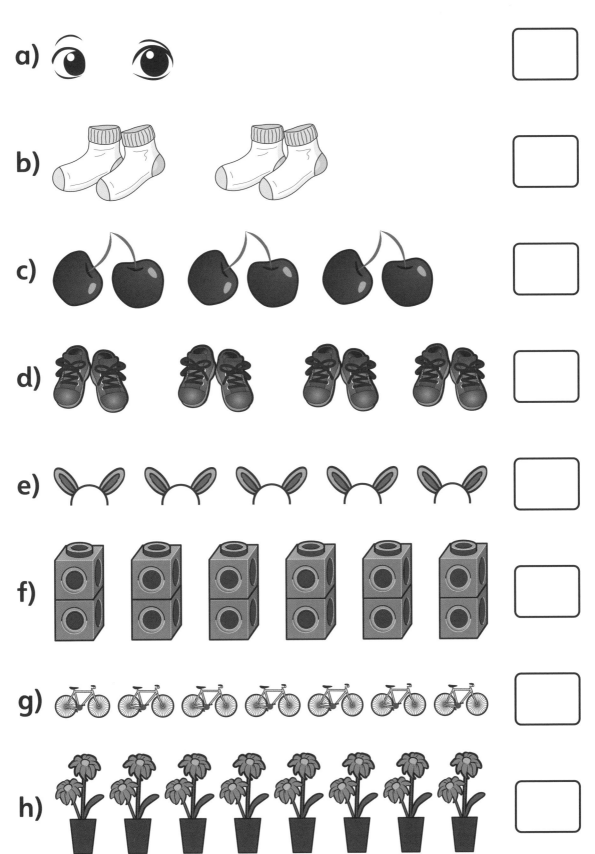

4 Complete the dot-to-dot picture by counting in 2s.

CHALLENGE

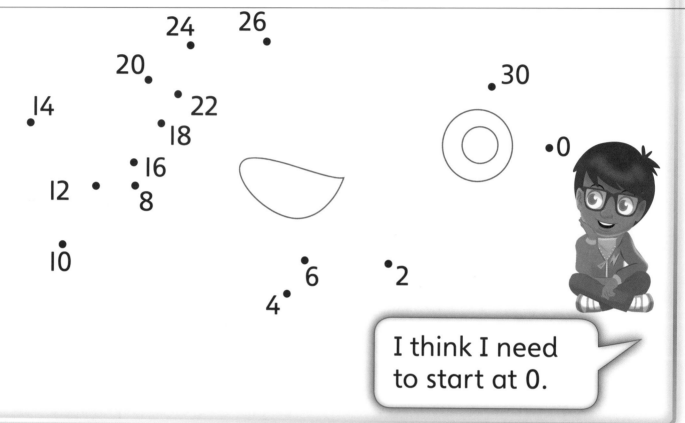

I think I need to start at 0.

Reflect

Count in 2s.

Shade in the 2s.

1	2	3	4	5	6	7	8	9	10
11	12	13	14	15	16	17	18	19	20
21	22	23	24	25	26	27	28	29	30
31	32	33	34	35	36	37	38	39	40
41	42	43	44	45	46	47	48	49	50

Count in 10s

1 Count in 10s.

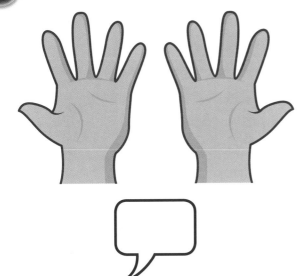

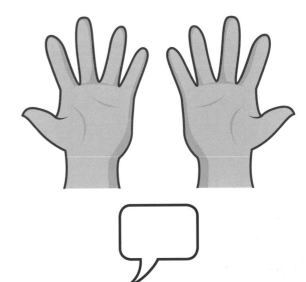

2 Count in 10s.

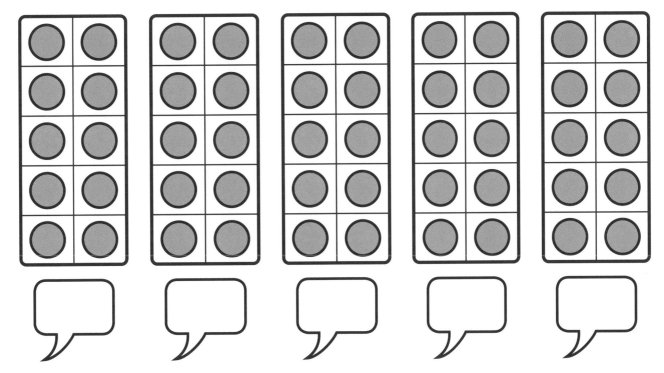

3 Shade in the 10s.

1	2	3	4	5	6	7	8	9	10
11	12	13	14	15	16	17	18	19	20
21	22	23	24	25	26	27	28	29	30
31	32	33	34	35	36	37	38	39	40
41	42	43	44	45	46	47	48	49	50

4 Count in 10s.

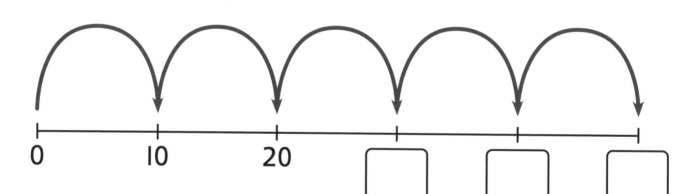

0   10   20

5 Count back in 10s.

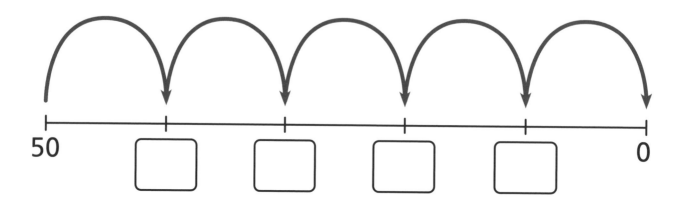

50   0

10

6 Shade the 10s.

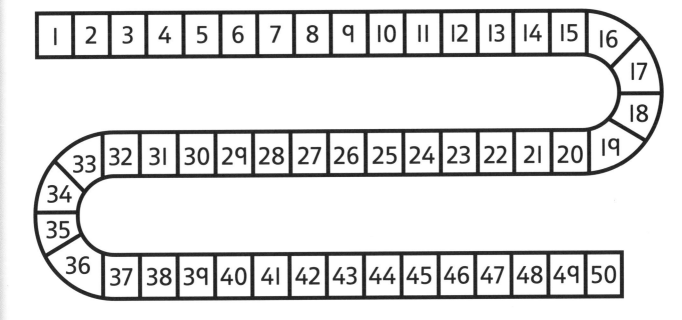

Now start again. Shade the 2s in a different colour.

Which numbers have you shaded twice?

Reflect

Practise counting in 10s with a partner.

Date: _____

Count in 5s

1 Count in 5s. Write the number of 5s in the box.

a)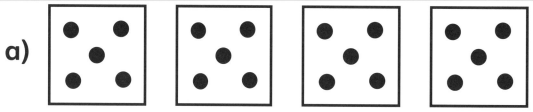

b)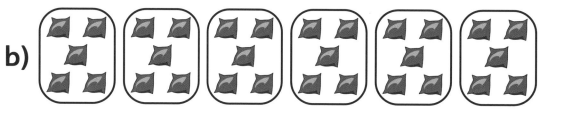

c)

2 Count in 5s. Write the number of 5s in the box.

3 Shade in all the 5s.

1	2	3	4	5	6	7	8	9	10
11	12	13	14	15	16	17	18	19	20
21	22	23	24	25	26	27	28	29	30
31	32	33	34	35	36	37	38	39	40
41	42	43	44	45	46	47	48	49	50

4 Count in 5s.

Write the numbers you get to in the boxes.

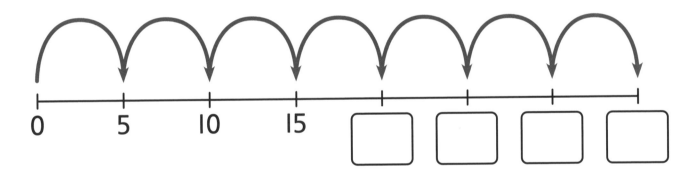

5 Count back in 5s from 50 to 20.

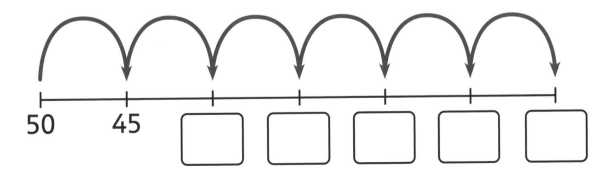

6 Shade the 5s.

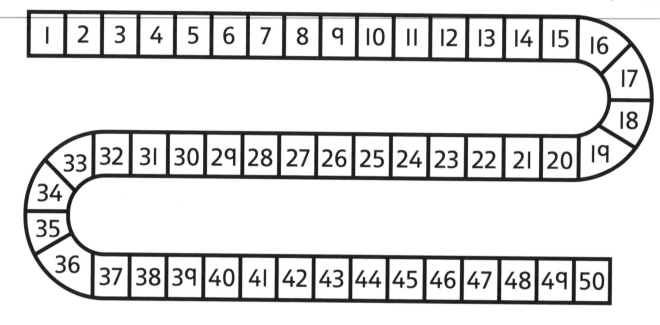

Now start again. Shade the 2s in a different colour.

Which numbers have you shaded twice?

Reflect

Practise counting in 5s with a partner.

Take it in turns to say each number.

→ Textbook 1C p20

Equal groups

1 Draw equal groups.

a)

b)

c)

d)

2 Draw 3 equal groups of 4 squares.

3 Count the equal groups.

a)

There are ☐ groups of 2 gloves.

b)

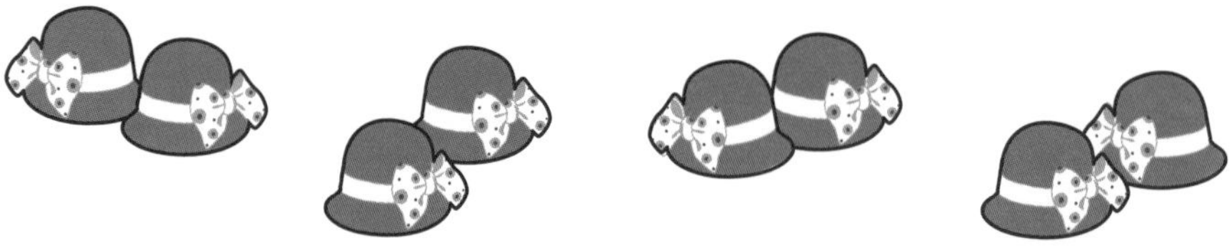

There are ☐ groups of 2 hats.

c)

There are ☐ groups of 2 scarves.

4 Complete the sentences.

CHALLENGE

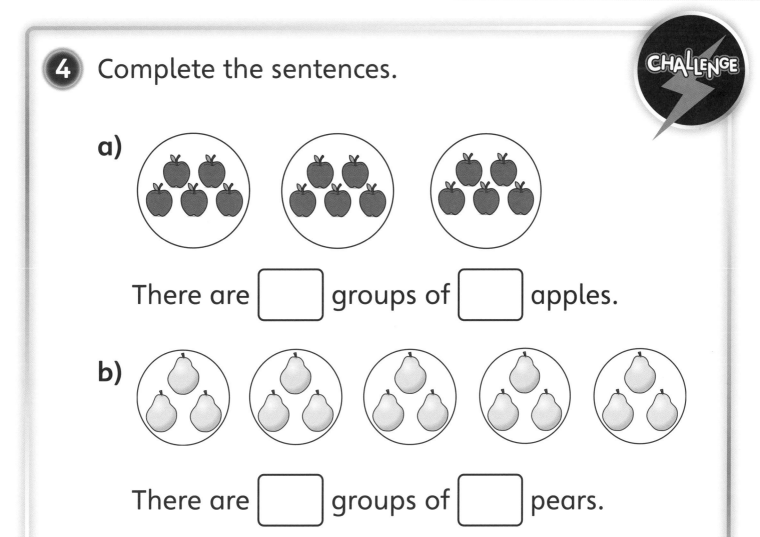

a)

There are ☐ groups of ☐ apples.

b)

There are ☐ groups of ☐ pears.

Reflect

Talk about these equal groups with a partner.

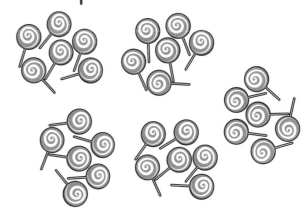

Date: _____

Add equal groups

1 **a)** How many wheels are there?

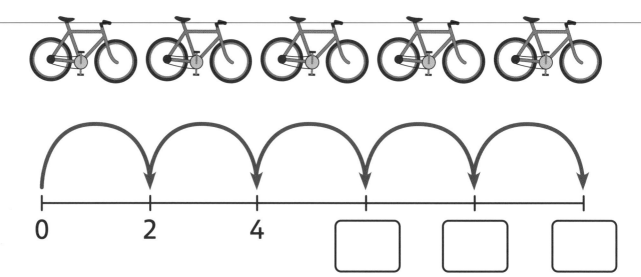

$2 + 2 + 2 + 2 + 2 =$ ☐

b) How many spots are there?

$5 + 5 + 5 + 5 =$ ☐

2 Add up the scores.

a)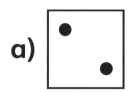

2 + 2 + 2 + 2 =

b)

5 + 5 + 5 + 5 + 5 =

3 Add up the number of cubes.

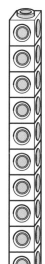 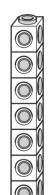 

10 + 10 + 10 + 10 =

19

4 Show that there is the same number of stickers on each sheet.

CHALLENGE

I know a quick way to count the stars.

Reflect

Show how you can count the shells.

Make arrays

1 Shade the rows.

Use a different colour for each row.

a)
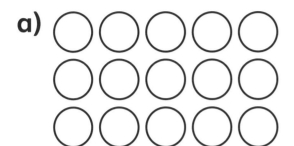

$5 + 5 + 5 =$ ☐

b)
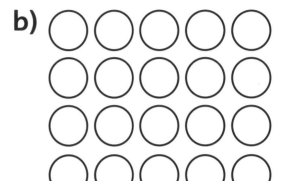

$5 + 5 + 5 + 5 =$ ☐

2 Shade the columns.

Use a different colour for each column.

a)

$2 + 2 + 2 + 2 =$ ☐

b)

$5 + 5 + 5 + 5 + 5 =$ ☐

21

3 Match the arrays to the descriptions.

△ ¦ △ ¦ △ ¦ △
△ ¦ △ ¦ △ ¦ △

| 4 columns |
| 2 △ in each column |

△ ¦ △ ¦ △
△ ¦ △ ¦ △
△ ¦ △ ¦ △
△ ¦ △ ¦ △

| 4 columns |
| 3 △ in each column |

△ ¦ △ ¦ △ ¦ △
△ ¦ △ ¦ △ ¦ △
△ ¦ △ ¦ △ ¦ △

| 3 columns |
| 4 △ in each column |

4 How many stars in each array?

a)

☐ + ☐ + ☐ = ☐

There are ☐ stars.

b)

☐ + ☐ + ☐ = ☐

There are ☐ stars.

5 Draw your own array with 10 in each row.

CHALLENGE

Reflect

I think I can do this in two ways.

Write an addition for this array.

Date: _____

Make doubles

1 Circle the dominoes that show a double.

2 Draw white counters to show doubles.

The first one has been done for you.

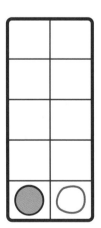 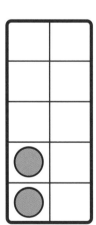 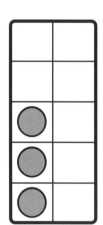 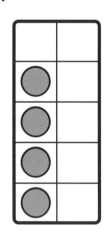 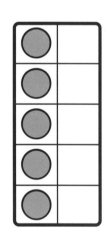

Fill in the missing numbers.

Double 1 is ☐ .   Double ☐ is ☐ .

Double 2 is ☐ .   Double ☐ is ☐ .

Double 3 is ☐ .

24

3 Complete the sentences.

a)

Double 4 is ⬜.

c)

Double ⬜ is 2.

b)

Double ⬜ is 10.

d)

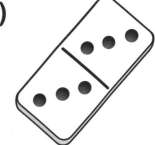

Double ⬜ is ⬜.

4 Work out double six.

Double 6 is ⬜.

5 Complete the doubles.

a) 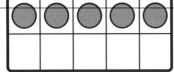 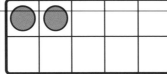 Double 7 is .

b) 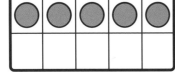 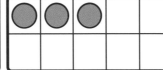 Double 8 is [ ].

c) 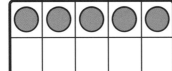 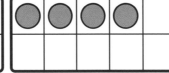 Double 9 is [ ].

d) 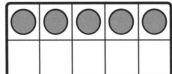 Double 10 is [ ].

Reflect

How many doubles can you and a partner remember?

Grouping

1 Circle groups of 2. Write the number of groups of 2.

a)

There are ⬚ groups of 2.

b)

There are ⬚ groups of 2.

c)

There are ⬚ groups of 2.

2 Circle groups of 3. Write the number of groups of 3.

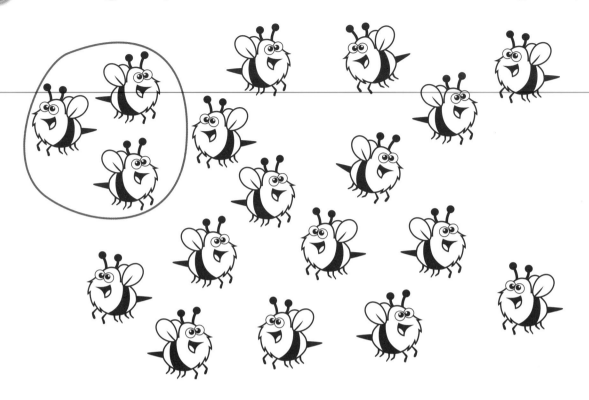

There are ☐ groups of 3.

3 Circle groups of 4. Write the number of groups of 4.

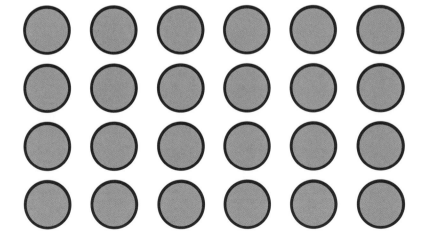

There are ☐ groups of 4.

4 Draw 15 people playing in groups of 5.

How many groups of 5 have you drawn?

CHALLENGE

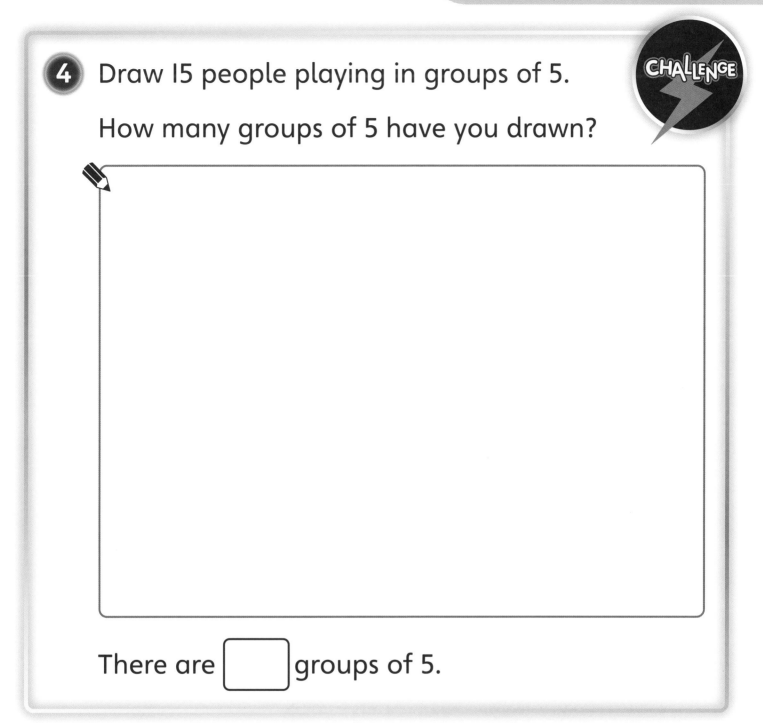

There are ☐ groups of 5.

Reflect

Use 20 cubes. Make equal groups of 5.

Work with a partner. Talk about what you have done.

Date: _____

Sharing

1 Share the apples between the 2 circles.

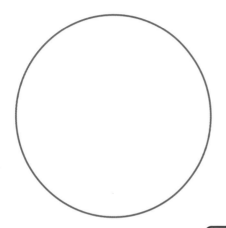 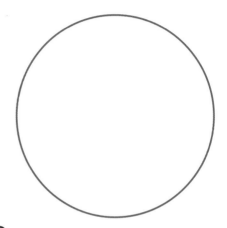

8 shared between 2 is ☐.

2 Share the bananas between the two circles.

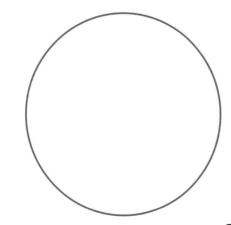 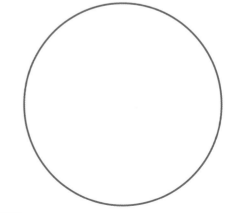

10 shared between 2 is ☐.

3 Share the triangles between the 3 circles.

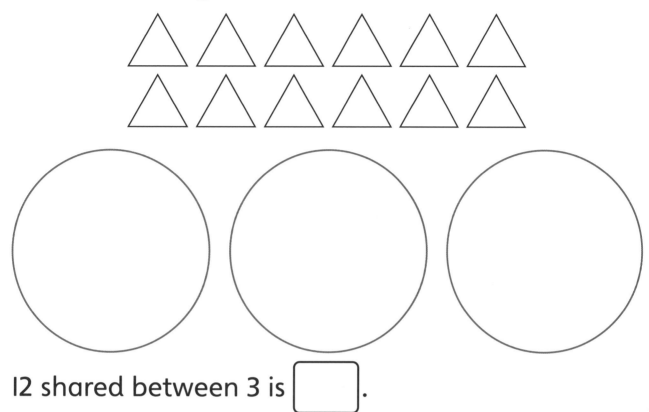

12 shared between 3 is [   ].

4 Share the stars between the 4 circles.

12 shared between 4 is [   ].

5 Complete the sentences.

CHALLENGE

a) ○○○○○
○○○○○
○○○○○
○○○○○

20 shared between 4 is ☐.

b) ○○○○○○○○○○
○○○○○○○○○○

20 shared between 10 is ☐.

Reflect

Share the toy cars equally between the children.

There are ☐ cars.

They are shared between ☐ children.

Each child gets ☐ cars.

Date: _____

End of unit check

My journal

This is double 10.

Joe

This is 10 groups of 2.

Sara

I can see 2 groups of 10.

Poppy

Who is correct?

Show their groups.

Power check

How do you feel about your work in this unit?

Power play

Draw a straight line in each box so that the dots are split into equal groups.

The first one has been done for you.

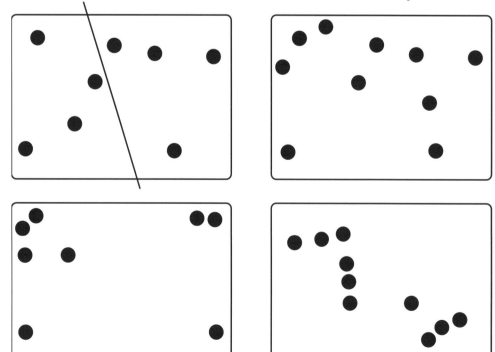

Date: _____

Recognise and find a half of a shape

1 Shade in one half of each shape.

↓ Textbook 1C p48

a)

b)

c)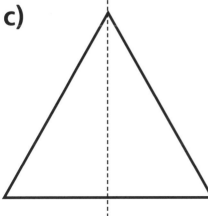

d)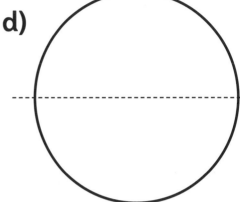

e)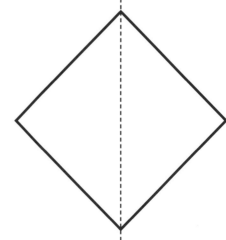

f)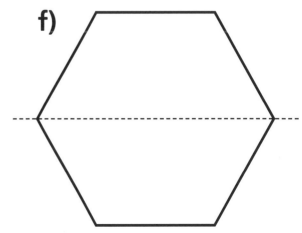

35

2 Shade in one half of each shape.

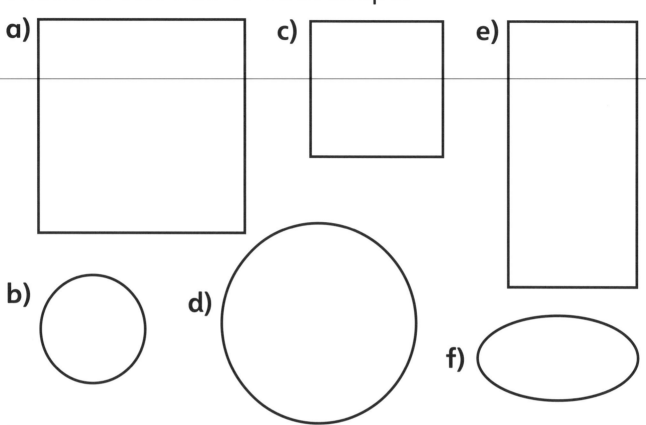

a)

c)

e)

b)

d)

f)

3 Tick the shapes that are half shaded.

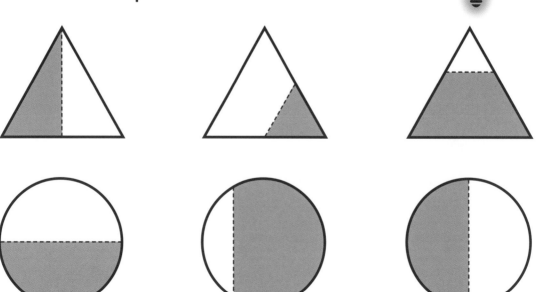

4 Draw an arrow half-way along the line.

_____

5 Draw the missing halves.

CHALLENGE

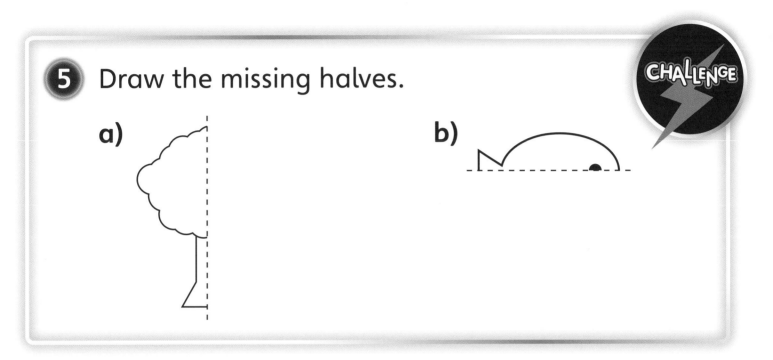

a)

b)

Reflect

Draw a picture to show half of a shape.

Date: _____

Recognise and find a half of a quantity

1 Shade in half of the items in each line.

a)

b)

c)

d)

2 Shade in half of the items in each question.

a)

c)

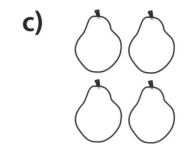

b)

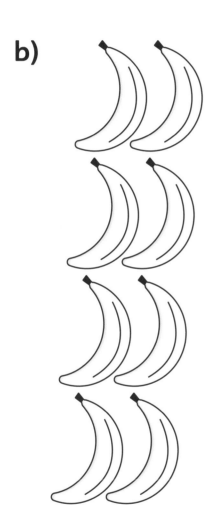

d)

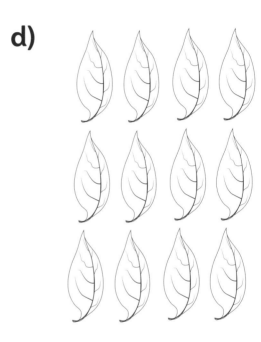

3 Find half of each number.

a)

Half of 2 is ☐.

b)

Half of 4 is ☐.

c)

Half of 6 is ☐.

d)

Half of 8 is ☐.

Reflect

Talk with a partner about double 5.

Talk to them about half of 10.

Recognise and find a quarter of a shape

1 Shade a quarter of each shape.

a) 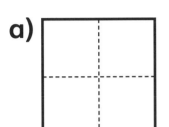 c) 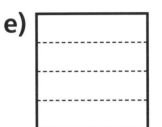 e) 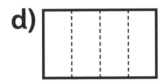 g)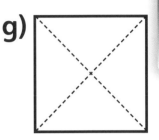

b) 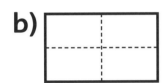 d) 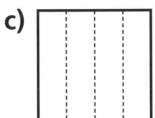 f) 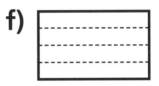 h)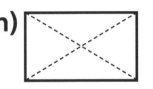

2 Shade a quarter of each shape.

a)

b) 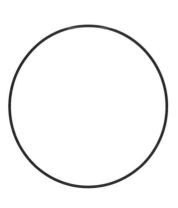 c) 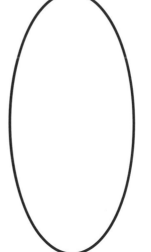 d)

↓ Textbook 1C p56

3 Tick the shapes that are a quarter shaded.

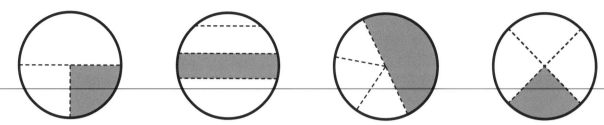

4 There are 4 painters.

They each paint a quarter of the wall.

Draw lines to split the wall into quarters.

Shade each quarter a different colour.

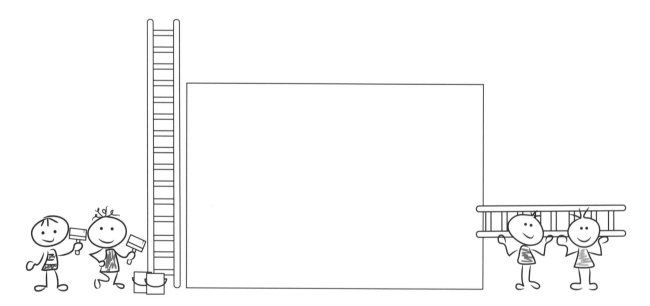

5 Split these shapes into quarters in two different ways.

CHALLENGE

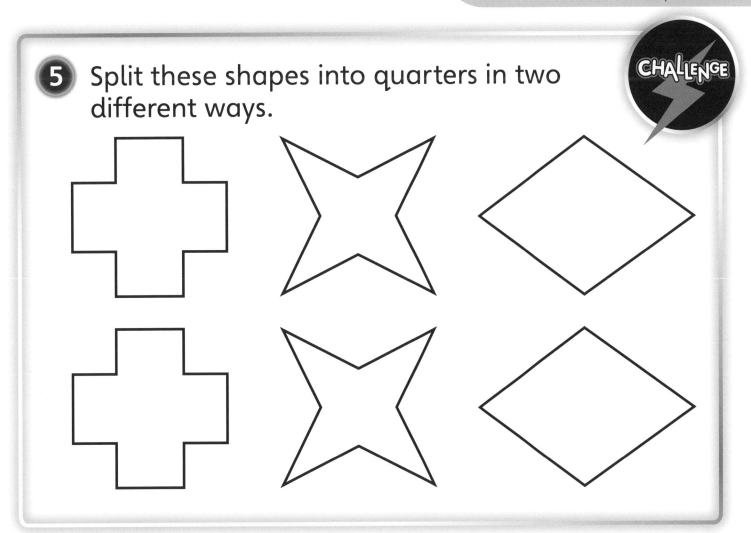

Reflect

Draw a picture to show one quarter of a shape.

Date: _____

Recognise and find a quarter of a quantity

1 Split these boxes into quarters.

a)

b)

2 Share these birds into quarters.

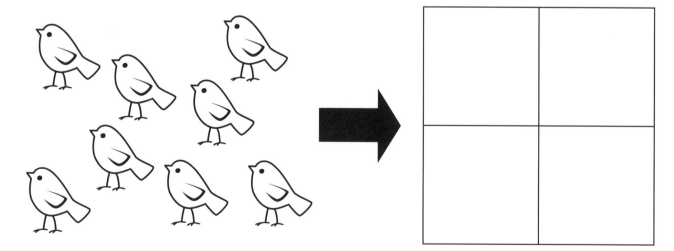

3 One quarter has been done. Draw the whole.

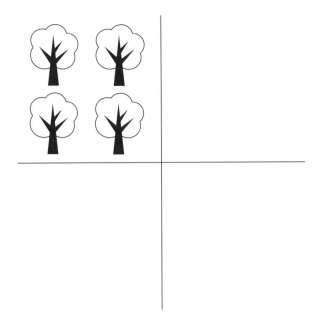

4 Tick the shapes that show quarters.

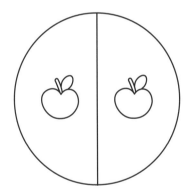

5 Share the stars into quarters.

Colour each quarter a different colour.

Reflect

Draw a picture of 12 shared into halves.

Now draw a picture of 12 shared into quarters.

End of unit check

My journal

Luke wants half of these strawberries.

Eva wants one quarter.

Luke works out half.

Eva gets stuck.

Explain why this might be.

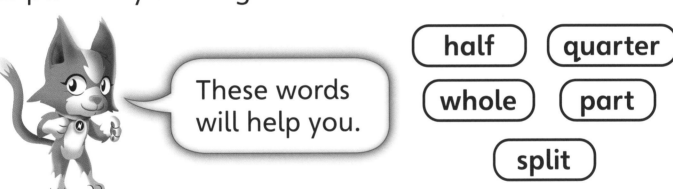

These words will help you.

| half | quarter |
| whole | part |
| split |

Power check

How do you feel about your work in this unit?

Textbook 1C p64

Date: _____

Power puzzle

Half of these squares have been shaded.

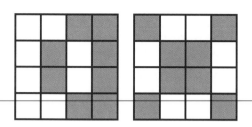

Shade half of these shapes.

Make different patterns.

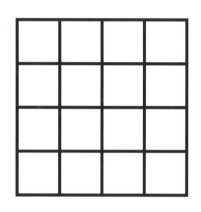

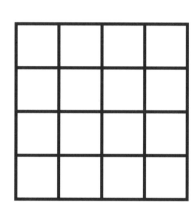

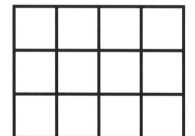

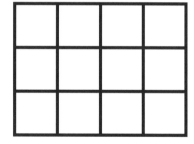

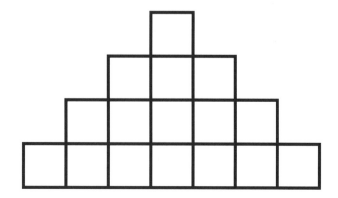

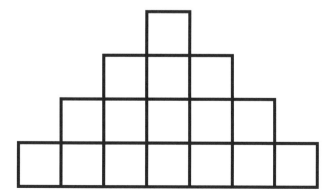

Date: _____

Describe turns

↓ Textbook 1C p68

1 **a)** Joe is facing the lion.

He makes a half turn.
Circle the object he is now facing.

b) Joe is facing the parrot.

He makes a half turn.
Circle the object he is now facing.

c) Joe is facing the elephant.

He makes a whole turn.
Circle the object he is now facing.

2 **a)** Em is facing the car.

She makes a quarter turn right.
Circle what she is facing now.

b) Em is facing the car.

She makes a quarter turn left.
Circle what she is facing now.

c) Em is facing the ball.

She makes 3 quarter turns right.
Circle what she is facing now.

3 Which does not describe the turn of the tractor?

CHALLENGE

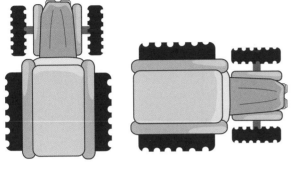

quarter turn right

half turn left

three-quarter turn left

Explain why.

_____

_____

_____

Reflect

Face a partner.

Follow these instructions.

1. Make a quarter turn to the left.

2. Make a half turn to the right.

3. Make 3 quarter turns to the right.

Where are you facing now?

51

Date: _____

Describe position – left and right

1 Shade in the **left** arrow.

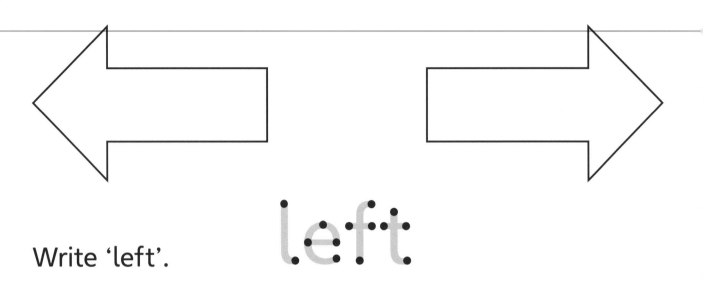

Write 'left'.

2 Shade in the **right** arrow.

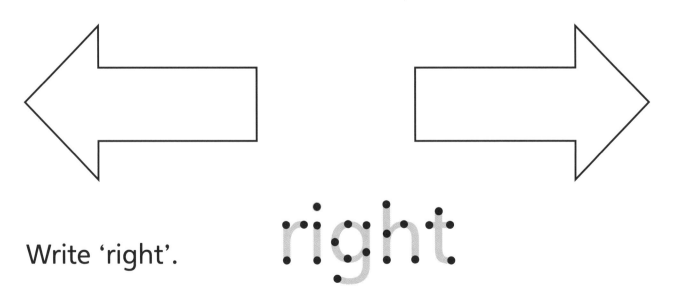

Write 'right'.

3 Circle the object on the left.

4 Circle the object on the right.

5 Here are 3 children.

a) Who is standing to the left of Joe?

_____

b) Who is standing to the right of Joe?

_____

6 **a)** Draw a dog to the left of a cat.

b) Draw a fish to the right of the cat.

CHALLENGE

Reflect

Practise lifting your left hand and right hand.

Say which hand you are lifting as you go. Ask a partner to check.

Make up a dance with left and right turns.
Show your partner.

Describe position – forwards and backwards

1 Move through the maze. Draw your route.

Talk about the left and right turns on the route.

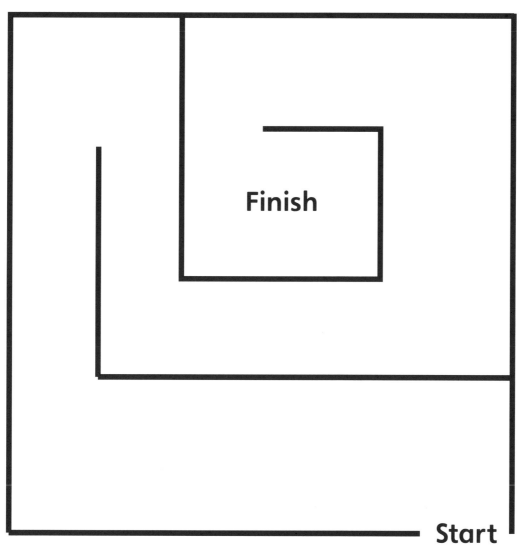

Finish

Start

I will use a toy to go through the maze.

Here is a map of a park.

Find different routes to get from one thing to another.

Use left and right turns and steps forwards and backwards. Describe your routes to a partner.

3 Draw your own map. Find different routes from one thing to another.

Describe your routes to a partner using left and right turns and steps forwards and backwards.

Reflect

Describe to a partner how to move from your seat in the classroom to the playground.

Date: _____

Describe position – above and below

1 Here is a grid of animals.

Circle **above** or **below**, **left** or **right** to make the sentences correct.

a) The 🐱 is above / below the 🐘 .

b) The 🐑 is to the left / right of the 🐕 .

c) The 🐯 is above / below the 🐁 and to

the left / right of the  .

2 Draw a 🌳 and a 🏠 in the correct spaces.

The 🌳 is above the 🪨.

The 🏠 is to the left of the 🚲.

3 Describe the position of the socks in three different ways.

hat	T-shirt	dress
shoes	socks	trousers

1. _____.

2. _____.

3. _____.

4 Here is a grid of letters.

Use the clues to find a four-letter word.

a	t	b
k	e	p
d	c	l

1. the letter between d and l   _____

2. the letter to the left of t   _____

3. the letter above d   _____

4. the letter on the middle row between k and p   _____

Reflect

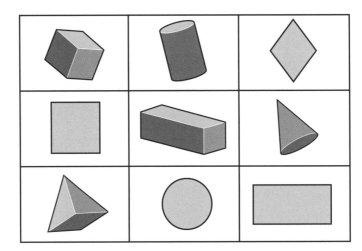

Choose a shape from the grid.

Describe the position of this shape to a partner.

Ask your partner to say which shape you chose.

Textbook 1C p84

Ordinal numbers

1 **a)** Circle the 1st apple.

b) Circle the 2nd tree.

c) Circle the 3rd frog.

d) Circle the 5th football.

2 Continue the pattern. Label the items 1st, 2nd, ...

_____ _____ _____ _____ _____ _____

3 There are 4 shapes in a line.

The 1st shape is a circle.
The 2nd shape is a square.
The 3rd shape is a triangle.
The 4th shape is circle.

Draw the shapes in order.

4 **a)** Circle the 3rd child from the left.

b) Circle the 3rd child from the right.

5 Fill in the number in the lock.

The 3rd digit is a 5.

The 4th digit is a 7.

The 1st digit is the same as the 4th.

The 2nd digit is 1 more than the 1st.

CHALLENGE

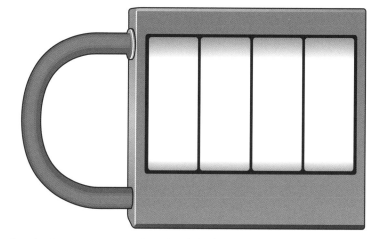

Reflect

What are the first four things you do in the morning?

- First, _____
- Second, _____
- Third, _____
- Fourth, _____

Date: _____

End of unit check

My journal

↑ Textbook 1C p88

Guide the mouse to the cheese.

Find more than one path.

Write the directions.

_____

_____

_____

_____

These words might help you.

forwards	backwards
left	right
half turn	quarter turn

Power check

How do you feel about your work in this unit?

Power puzzle

Work out the name of each person.

Anya is to the left of the person wearing a hat.

Hassan is below Anya.

Quinn is above the person to the right of Katie.

Maya is on the top row.

If Bob looks up he can see Quinn.

Date: ______________________

→ Textbook 1C p92

Count from 50 to 100

1 Write in the missing numbers.

a)

51	52	53	54	55	56	57	58	59	

b)

61	62	63	64	65	66	67			

c)

71	72	73	74	75					

d)

81	82	83	84						

e)

91	92	93							

Now point and count with a partner.

2 Count up to 100. Write in the missing numbers.

1	2	3	4	5	6	7	8	9	10
11	12	13	14	15	16	17	18	19	20
21	22		24	25	26	27	28	29	30
	32	33	34	35	36	37	38	39	40
41	42	43	44	45	46	47		49	50
51	52	53	54		56	57	58	59	
61	62	63	64	65	66	67	68	69	70
71	72	73		75	76	77	78	79	80
81	82		84	85	86	87	88	89	90
91	92	93	94	95		97		99	100

3 Complete the number tracks.

a)

85	86	87							94

b)

90	89	88							81

4 Complete the dot-to-dot picture.
Follow the numbers back from 100 to 60.

 **CHALLENGE**

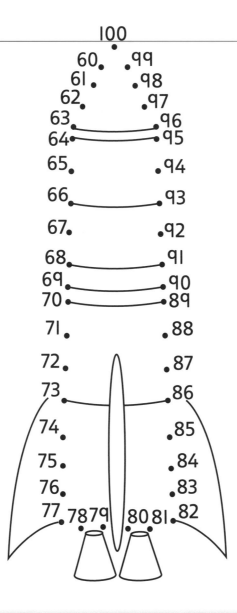

Reflect

Which do you find easier? Counting on or counting back? Discuss with a partner.

10s to 100

1 Write in the missing numbers.

1	2	3	4	5	6	7	8	9	
11	12	13	14	15	16	17	18	19	
21	22	23	24	25	26	27	28	29	
31	32	33	34	35	36	37	38	39	
41	42	43	44	45	46	47	48	49	
51	52	53	54	55	56	57	58	59	
61	62	63	64	65	66	67	68	69	
71	72	73	74	75	76	77	78	79	
81	82	83	84	85	86	87	88	89	
91	92	93	94	95	96	97	98	99	

2 Complete the number track.

10	20	30	40						100

3 Count in 10s. Write how many 10s there are in each box.

a)

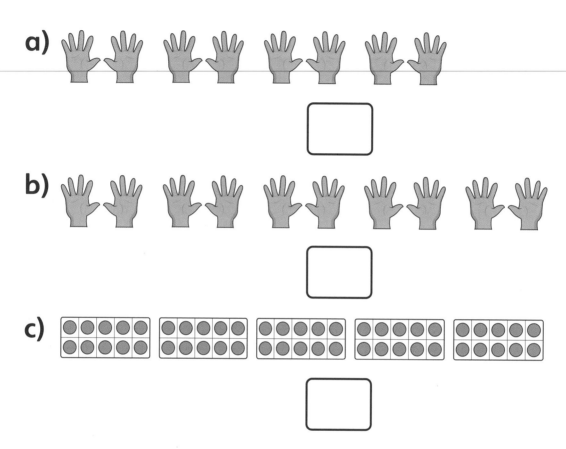

b)

c)

4 How many eggs are there?

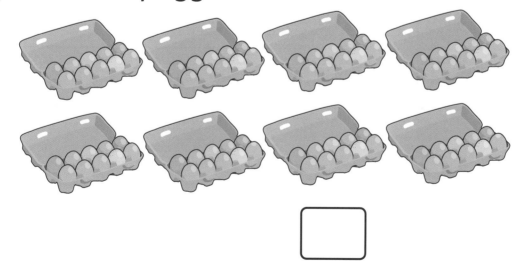

5 Count in 10s.

a) How many sweets are there?

b) How many pegs are there?

c) Circle 50 pens.

Reflect

Count on in 10s.

Show 10s on your fingers as you count.

Date: _____

Partition into 10s and 1s

1 Count in 10s then in 1s.

a)

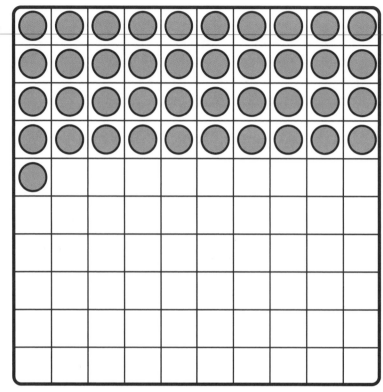

b)

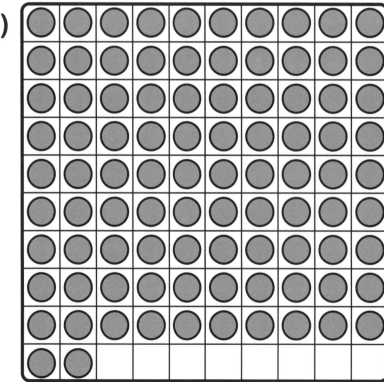

2 How many counters are there?

a)

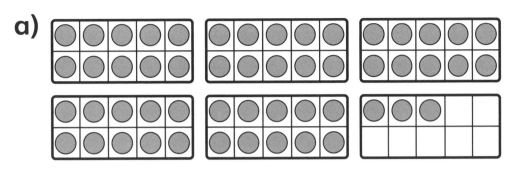

There are ☐ counters.

b)

There are ☐ counters.

3 How many pencils are there?

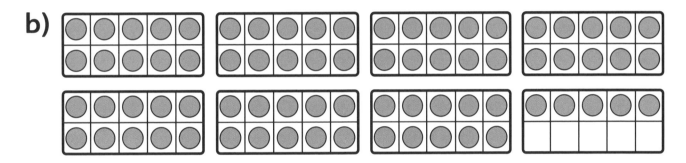

There are ☐ pencils.

CHALLENGE

4 How many buttons are there?

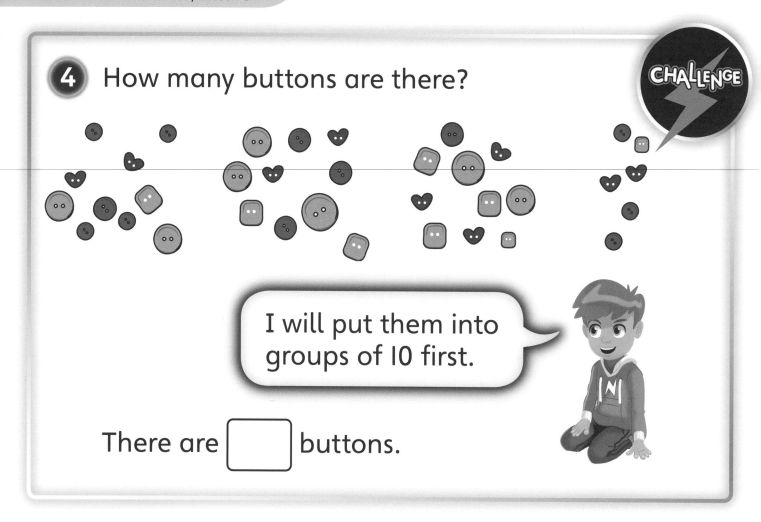

I will put them into groups of 10 first.

There are [ ] buttons.

Reflect

Talk with a partner about the 10s and 1s. What is this number?

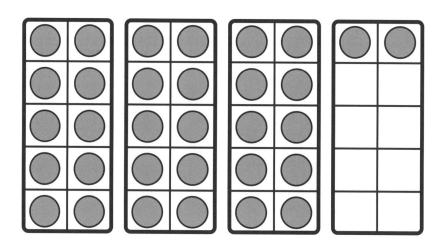

↓ Textbook 1C p104

Number line to 100

1 Write in the missing numbers.

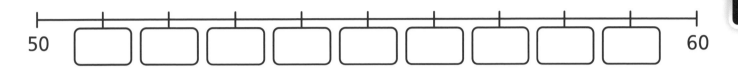

2 What are these numbers?

a)

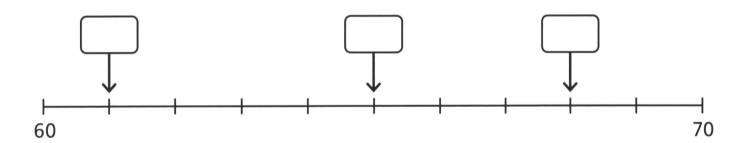

b)

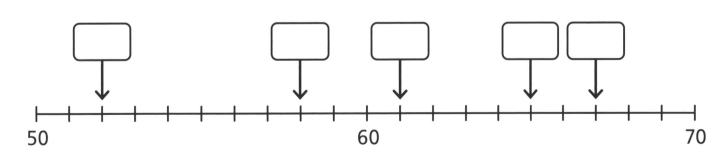

3 Join each number to the right place on the number line. One has been done for you.

a)   42   43   45   48

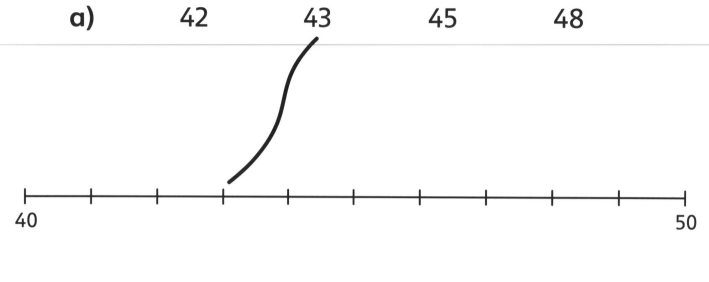

40   50

b) 72   75   78   82   89

70   80   90

4 Complete the number lines.

a)

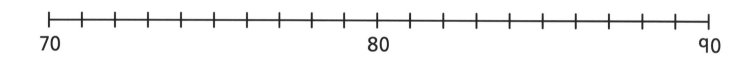

0   10   20   30 ⬚ ⬚ ⬚ ⬚ ⬚ ⬚ 100

b)

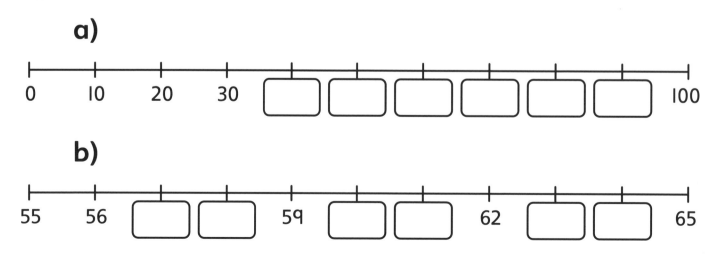

55   56 ⬚ ⬚ 59 ⬚ ⬚ 62 ⬚ ⬚ 65

5 Join each number to the right place on the number line. One has been done for you. **CHALLENGE**

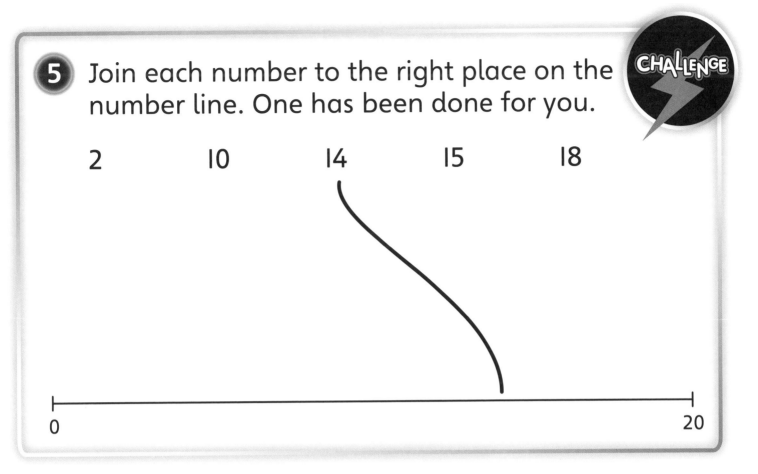

Reflect

Draw your own number line. Show 22 on your line.

Date: _____

One more and one less

1 What is one more than each number?

a)

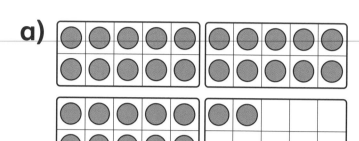

b)

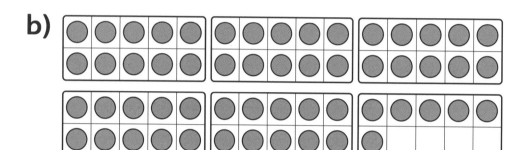

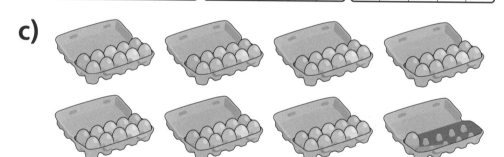

c)

2 Max has made the number 45.

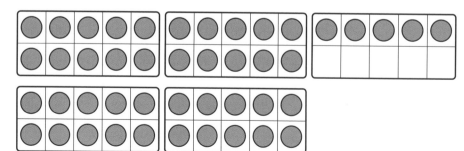

What is one less than Max's number?

3 Find one more and one less.

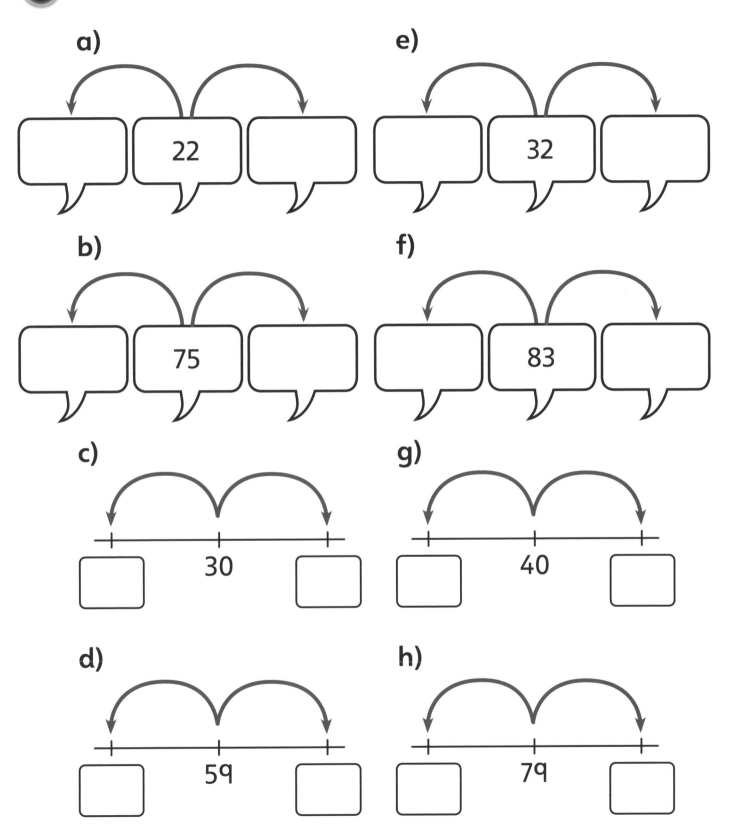

a)

22

e)

32

b)

75

f)

83

c)

30

g)

40

d)

59

h)

79

4 Complete the missing numbers.

a)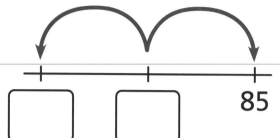

☐ ☐ 85

b)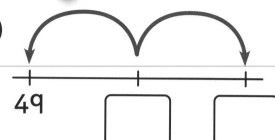

49 ☐ ☐

5

a) $40 + 1 = \boxed{}$

$40 - 1 = \boxed{}$

b) $37 + 1 = \boxed{}$

$37 - 1 = \boxed{}$

c) $48 + 1 = \boxed{}$

$48 - 1 = \boxed{}$

d) $99 + 1 = \boxed{}$

$99 - 1 = \boxed{}$

Reflect

Play a game with a partner.

Your partner says a number. You say one more.

Play a new game with a partner.

Your partner says a number. You say one less.

Compare numbers

1 Shade in all the numbers greater than 54.

51	52	53	54	55	56	57	58	59	60

2 Write the word 'greater' or 'less' to complete the sentences.

a)

31	32	33	34	35	36	37	38	39	40

32 is _____ than 39.

b)

41	42	43	44	45	46	47	48	49	50

42 is _____ than 41.

c)

61	62	63	64	65	66	67	68	69	70

65 is _____ than 66.

d)

91	92	93	94	95	96	97	98	99	100

100 is _____ than 99.

3

1	2	3	4	5	6	7	8	9	10
11	12	13	14	15	16	17	18	19	20
21	22	23	24	25	26	27	28	29	30
31	32	33	34	35	36	37	38	39	40
41	42	43	44	45	46	47	48	49	50
51	52	53	54	55	56	57	58	59	60
61	62	63	64	65	66	67	68	69	70
71	72	73	74	75	76	77	78	79	80
81	82	83	84	85	86	87	88	89	90
91	92	93	94	95	96	97	98	99	100

Choose < or > to complete the number sentences.

a) 38 ◯ 31

b) 22 ◯ 25

c) 31 ◯ 26

d) 85 ◯ 25

e) 26 ◯ 38

f) 85 ◯ 86

Remember that < means less
than and > means greater than.

4 Put a different digit in each box to make the number sentence correct.

6	7	<	6	

6		<	6	7

5	7	<		8

Reflect

Put a number in each box to make the number sentence correct.

67 > ☐   67 < ☐

☐ < 67   ☐ > 67

1	2	3	4	5	6	7	8	9	10
11	12	13	14	15	16	17	18	19	20
21	22	23	24	25	26	27	28	29	30
31	32	33	34	35	36	37	38	39	40
41	42	43	44	45	46	47	48	49	50
51	52	53	54	55	56	57	58	59	60
61	62	63	64	65	66	67	68	69	70
71	72	73	74	75	76	77	78	79	80
81	82	83	84	85	86	87	88	89	90
91	92	93	94	95	96	97	98	99	100

Date: _____

End of unit check

My journal

You have a target number of 75.

Make it	Describe it 75 is made up of _____ _____	Break it apart 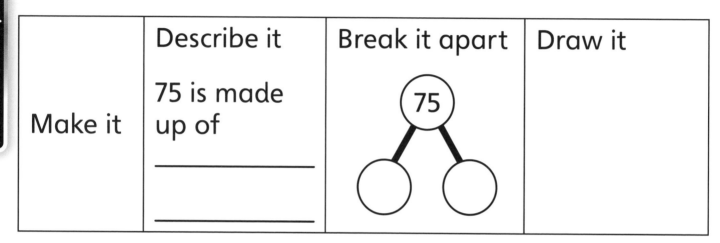	Draw it

I will try it with different target numbers.

These words might help you.

more   less

tens   ones

Power check

How do you feel about your work in this unit?

Power play

A game for 2 to 4 players.

6	7	4	6	3	1
9	5	2	8	3	7
8	1	0	1	5	6
4	4	3	0	1	7
3	2	8	2	9	8
5	7	4	7	3	0

Round 1

Shade in a 2-digit number on the square.

It can go left to right or downwards.

$\boxed{8\ \ 2} = 82$ or $\boxed{\begin{array}{c} 8 \\ \hline 4 \end{array}} = 84$

The player with the larger number scores a point.

Round 2

Shade in another 2-digit number on the square.

You may not shade a square more than once.

The player with the smaller number scores a point.

Repeat from the start of Round 1 until a player has got 4 points.

Date: _____

Recognise coins

 a) Circle the 10 pence coin.

b) Circle the 1 pound coin.

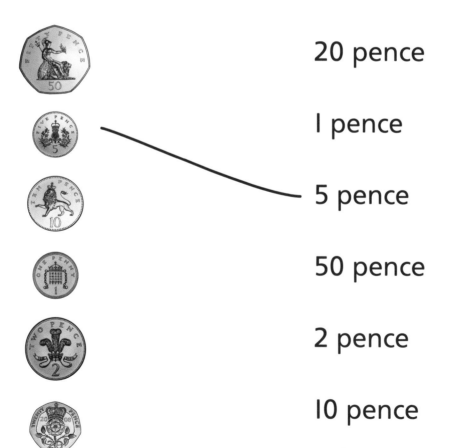 **2** Match the coins to the correct names.

20 pence

1 pence

5 pence

50 pence

2 pence

10 pence

Pence: 1 2 5 10 20 50

3 Here are some coins.

How many of each type of coin can you see?

a) There are ☐ 10 pence coins.

b) There are ☐ 20 pence coins.

c) There are ☐ 2 pound coins.

4 Draw an arrow to show where each coin should go.

Less than 10 pence		More than 10 pence
	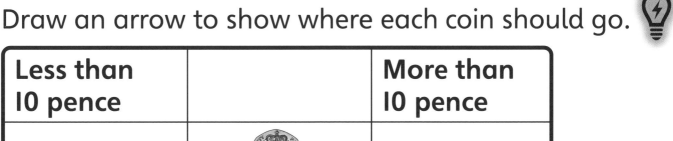	

5 Complete the table.

Circle the correct coins and fill in the gaps.

The first row has been done for you.

CHALLENGE

	5 pence	More than 2 pence
	20 pence	Less than _____
	☐ pence	More than _____
	☐ pence	Less than 20 pence

Reflect

Ask a partner to think of a coin.

What coin is your partner thinking of?

You can ask them three questions about it.

Use the key to help you.

Pence: 1 2 5 10 20 50

Date: _____

Recognise notes

↓ Textbook 1C p124

1 Match each note to its correct amount.

20 pound note

50 pound note

5 pound note

10 pound note

2 Circle the 10 pound notes.

Pounds: 1 2 5 10 20 50

3 How many of each note are there?

a) There are ⬚ 5 pound notes.

b) There are ⬚ 10 pound notes.

c) There are ⬚ 20 pound notes.

d) There are ⬚ 50 pound notes.

4 Use <, > or = to complete the sentences.

a) ◯ 10 pounds

b) 50 pounds ◯

c)  ◯

Pence: 1 2 5 10 20 50

5 Charlie thinks these notes are in order from greatest value to least value.

Tell a partner whether he is correct or not.

Reflect

Circle all the real notes.

Tell a partner which notes are not real.

Date: _____

Count in coins

1 How much is each group of coins worth?

a)  ☐ pence

b)  ☐ pence

c)  ☐ pence

d)  ☐ pence

2 Draw more coins to match the amounts.

a) 6 pence in 1 pence coins

b) 10 pence in 2 pence coins

Pence: 1 2 5  10 20 50

3 **a)** Circle coins worth 30 pence.

b) Circle coins worth 30 pence.

c) Circle coins worth 10 pence.

4 Use **more than**, **less than** or **the same as** to complete each number sentence.

a) is worth _____   .

b)   is worth _____   .

c)   is worth _____ .

5 Lucy has 6 silver coins.

Amy has 3 silver coins.

They have the same amount of money.

Which coins do they have?

CHALLENGE

I wonder which coins are silver. I will look at some real coins.

Reflect

Use 1 pence coins, 2 pence coins, 5 pence coins and 10 pence coins.

How many ways can you make 20 pence?

Use only one type of coin each time.

Pence: 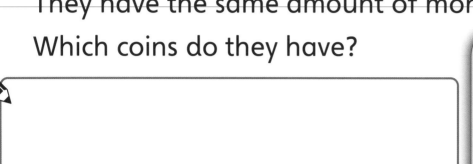 1 2 5 10 20 50

Date: _____

End of unit check

My journal

How many ways can you make 50 pence using

 , and  ?

You can use each coin more than once.

These words will help you.

pence   coin

five   ten   two

is equal to

Power check

How do you feel about your work in this unit?

Power play

Get into pairs or teams.

The first team chooses up to 5 of **one** kind of coin from  , and .

The second team asks questions to find out the total amount.

The first team can only answer yes or no.

Example:

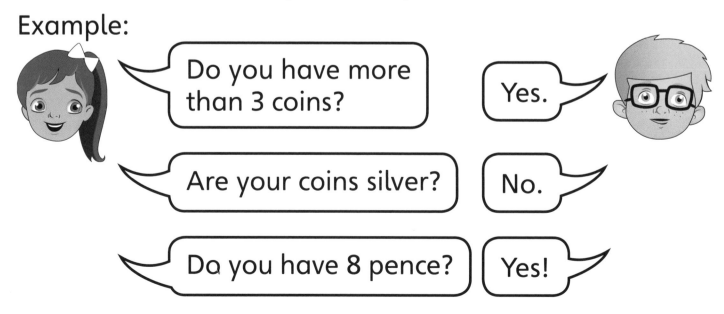

Do you have more than 3 coins?

Yes.

Are your coins silver?

No.

Da you have 8 pence?

Yes!

Date: _____

Before and after

Textbook 1C p136

 In each pair, circle the picture that comes after the other.

a)

b)

c)

97

2 In each pair, circle the picture that comes after the other.

a)

b)

3 Put these pictures in the correct order.

Number them 1 to 3 to show the correct order.

4 **a)** Tell a partner what might have happened before this.

b) Tell your partner what might happen after this.

Reflect

What things did you do before school today?

What things will you do after school today?

Date: _____

Days of the week

 a) Shade in the day today.

Sunday	Monday	Tuesday	Wednesday

Thursday	Friday	Saturday

b) Shade in the day yesterday.

Sunday	Monday	Tuesday	Wednesday

Thursday	Friday	Saturday

c) Shade in the day tomorrow.

Sunday	Monday	Tuesday	Wednesday

Thursday	Friday	Saturday

d) How many days are there in a week? [ ]

2 Which day comes next?

Wednesday	Thursday	Friday	

Circle your answer.

Monday   Saturday   Sunday

3 Find all the days of the week. Some go down the grid. The first one has been done for you.

S	U	F	R	I	D	A	Y	W
A	P	E	U	J	K	L	E	E
T	H	U	R	S	D	A	Y	D
U	M	U	A	E	L	O	P	N
R	D	I	H	X	J	E	K	E
D	M	O	N	D	A	Y	S	S
A	J	S	U	N	D	A	Y	D
Y	B	G	G	W	U	F	T	A
C	V	T	U	E	S	D	A	Y

4 Say or write the days that come between:

a)

Monday		Wednesday

b)

Thursday		Saturday

5 This is what Noah did this week.

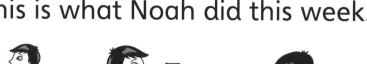

Sunday   Monday   Tuesday   Wednesday

Thursday   Friday   Saturday

Tell a partner:

a) What Noah did today?

b) What Noah did yesterday?

c) What Noah did the day after Friday?

d) What Noah did two days before Wednesday?

Reflect

Tell a partner the days of the week in order.

Do you know them all?

Can you write any of them?

Months of the year

1 **a)** Shade in the month it is now.

January	February	March	April
May	June	July	August
September	October	November	December

b) Shade in the month before.

January	February	March	April
May	June	July	August
September	October	November	December

c) Shade in the month you were born in.

January	February	March	April
May	June	July	August
September	October	November	December

2 Say or write the next month.

February	March	April	

3 Say or write the months that come between:

a)

June		August

b)

October		December

4 **a)** When is Gita's birthday?

_____

_____

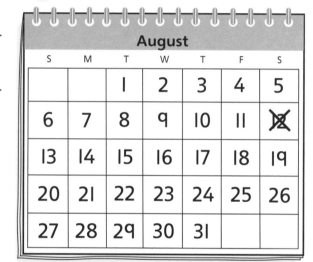

b) Lee's birthday is 25 March.

Put a cross on Lee's birthday.

5 Number the months in the correct order.
The month that comes first will be number 1.

CHALLENGE

January ☐

February ☐

May ☐

March ☐

April ☐

July ☐

August ☐

June ☐

November ☐

September ☐

October ☐

December ☐

I used a calendar to help me.

Reflect

Name all the months in the year.

Can you say them in order?

Date: _____

Tell the time to the hour

1 Match the times to the clocks.

12 o'clock

8 o'clock

1 o'clock

2 What time is it?

a)

[ ] o'clock

b)

[ ] o'clock

c)

[ ] o'clock

3 Draw the times.

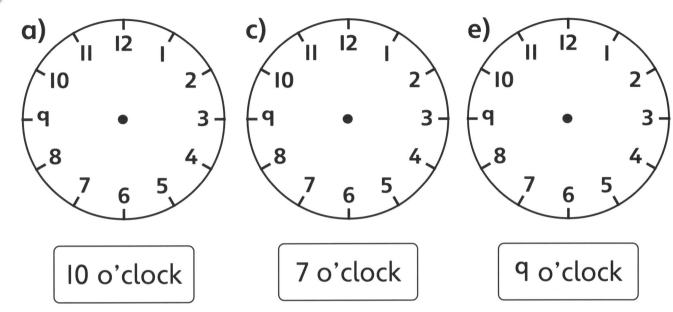

a)

10 o'clock

c)

7 o'clock

e)

9 o'clock

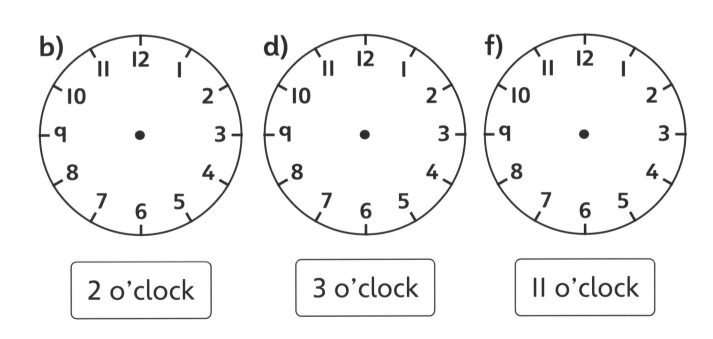

b)

2 o'clock

d)

3 o'clock

f)

11 o'clock

4 Who is correct? Circle their name.

The minute hand is pointing to the 12, so it is 12 o'clock.

The hour hand is pointing to the 5, so it is 5 o'clock.

Oliver

Kat

5 The minute and hour hand are both pointing to 12.

CHALLENGE

What time is it? Tell a partner what you do at this time of the day.

_____

Reflect

A clock shows 4 o'clock.

Draw it.

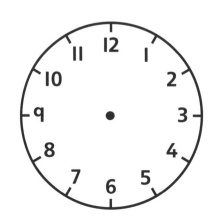

Tell the time to the half hour

Textbook 1C p152

1 Match the times to the clocks.

half past 5

half past 8

half past 6

half past 7

2 What time is it?

a)

half past ☐

c)

half past ☐

b)

half past ☐

d)

half past ☐

3 Draw the times.

a)

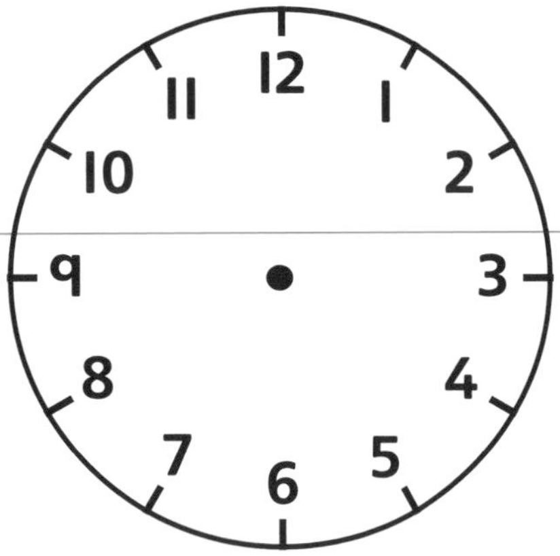

half past 2

c)

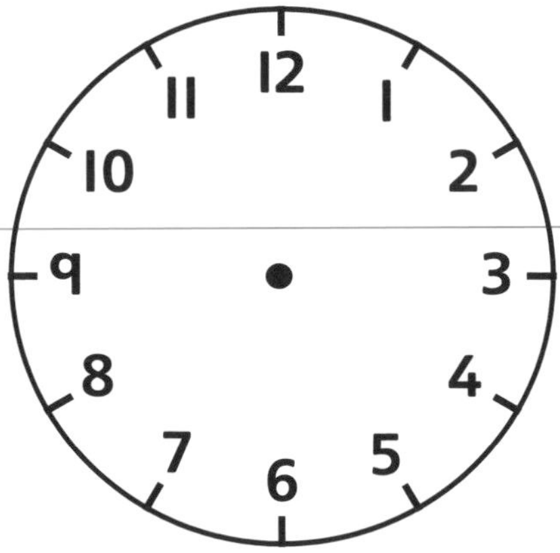

half past 3

b)

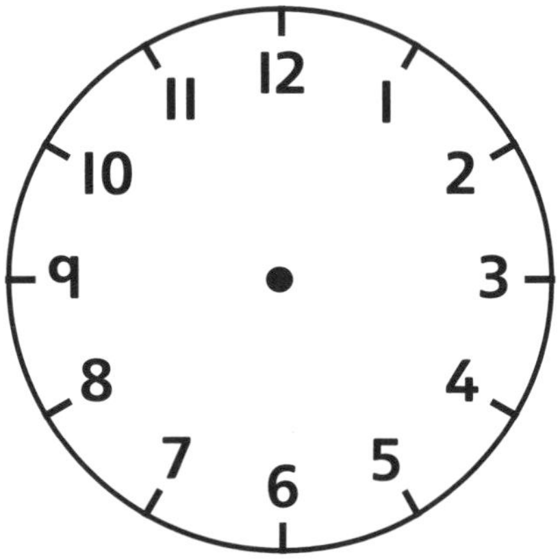

half past 4

d)

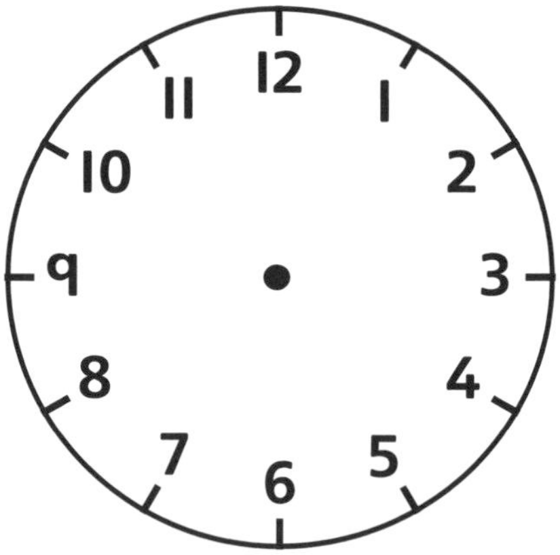

half past 9

4 Is Maya correct?

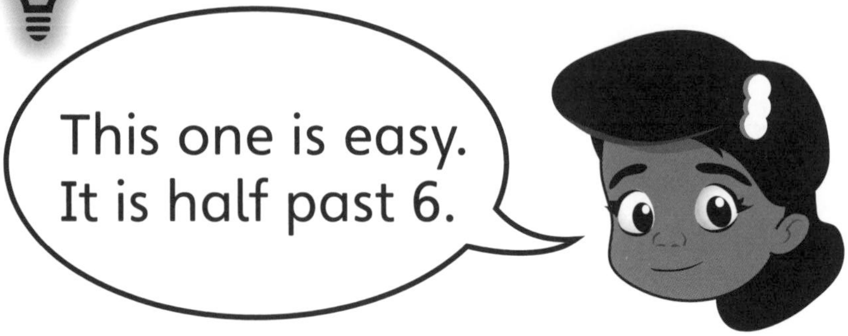

This one is easy. It is half past 6.

Circle the correct answer.   Yes   No

5

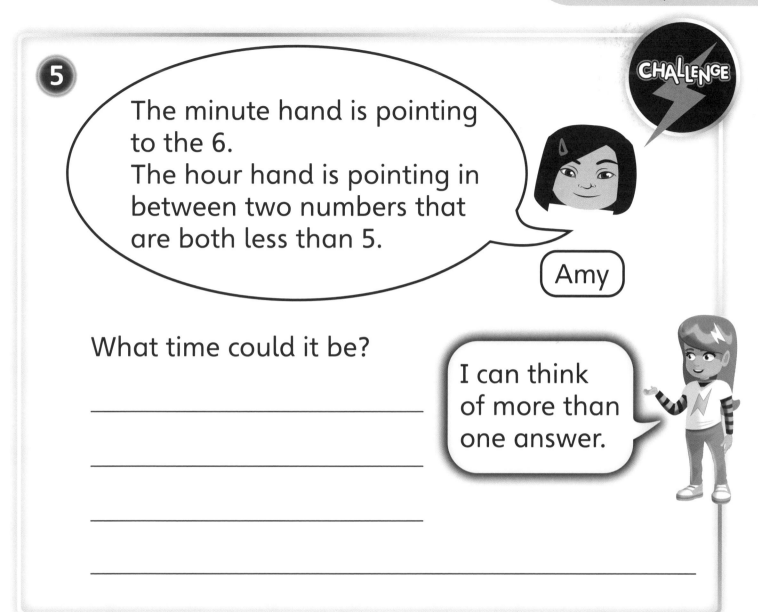

The minute hand is pointing to the 6.
The hour hand is pointing in between two numbers that are both less than 5.

Amy

CHALLENGE

What time could it be?

I can think of more than one answer.

_____

_____

_____

_____

Reflect

A clock shows half past 7.

Draw it.

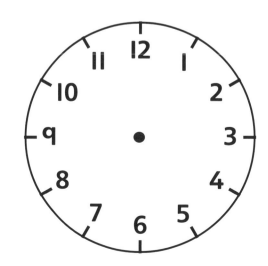

Date: _____

End of unit check

My journal

→ Textbook 1C p156

Look at these two clocks.

What is the same?

What is different?

These words might help you.

minute hand

hour hand

half past

Power check

How do you feel about your work in this unit?

Power play

Clever clocks

Draw a clock showing one of these times.
Show a partner.

5 o'clock	half past 10	7 o'clock	2 o'clock
half past 7	1 o'clock	half past 12	11 o'clock
half past 1	6 o'clock	half past 5	half past 6
12 o'clock	half past 2	10 o'clock	half past 11

If your partner tells you the correct time, they should shade that time in.

Take it in turns to make and name the different times.

Who shades in the most times?

My Power Points

Colour in the ☆ to show what you have learnt.

Colour in the ☺ if you feel happy about what you have learnt.

Unit 11

I can ...

☆ ☺ Count in 2s, 5s and 10s

☆ ☺ Make equal groups and add them to find the total

☆ ☺ Make an array

☆ ☺ Double a number

☆ ☺ Understand the difference between grouping and sharing

Unit 12

I can ...

☆ ☺ Find half of a shape

☆ ☺ Find half of a small number

☆ ☺ Find a quarter of a shape

☆ ☺ Find a quarter of a quantity

Unit 13

I can …

☆ ☺ Talk about half, quarter and three-quarter turns

☆ ☺ Use words like up, down, left and right to say where something is

☆ ☺ Understand 1st, 2nd, 3rd …

Unit 14

I can …

☆ ☺ Count in 10s to 100

☆ ☺ Use a 100 square to look for a pattern

☆ ☺ Use a number line to 100

☆ ☺ Understand one more and one less

☆ ☺ Compare two numbers and say which is more and less

Unit 15

I can …

☆ ☺ Say the name of any coin

☆ ☺ Say the name of any note

☆ ☺ Count in coins

Unit 16

I can ...

☆ ☺ Use the words before and after to talk about time

☆ ☺ Find the day of the week and the date on a calendar

☆ ☺ Read an o'clock time and a half-past time on a clock

Look at what you put on the first page. Did you do what you said? Could you do even better?

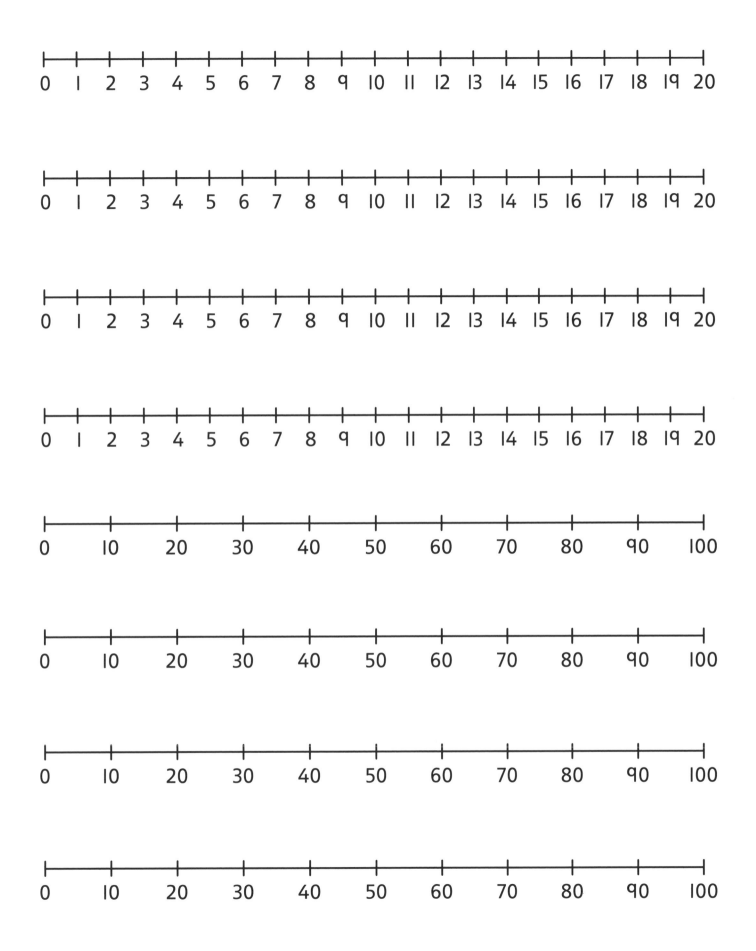

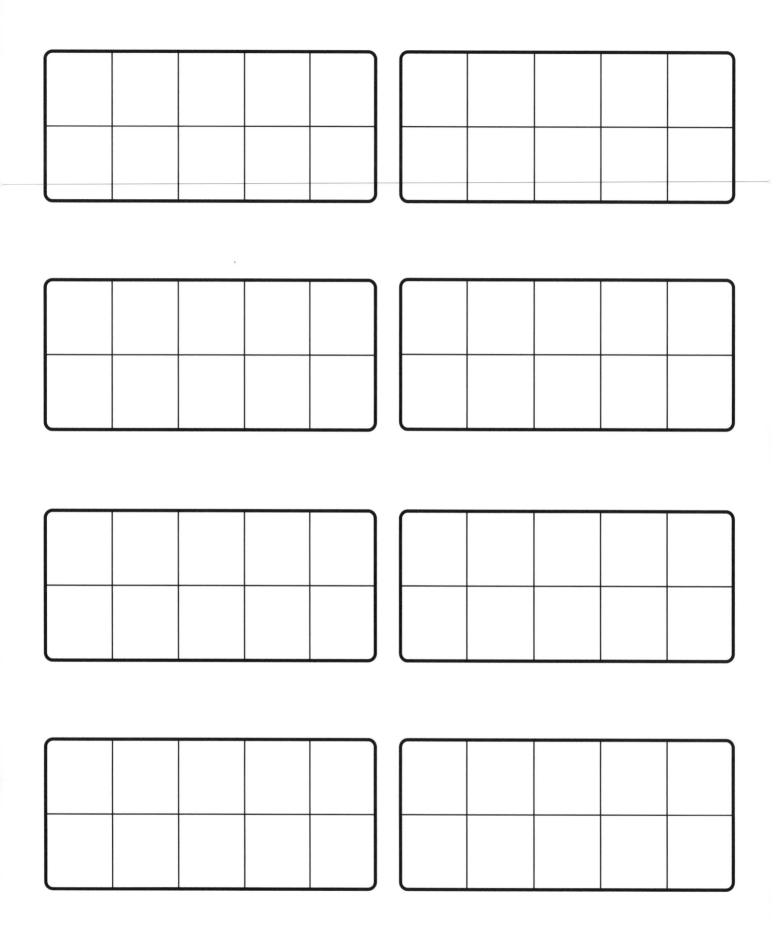

Published by Pearson Education Limited, 80 Strand, London, WC2R 0RL.

www.pearsonschools.co.uk

Text © Pearson Education Limited 2017, 2023
Edited by Pearson and Florence Production Ltd
First edition edited by Pearson, Little Grey Cells Publishing Services and Haremi Ltd
Designed and typeset by Pearson and PDQ Digital Media Solutions Ltd
First edition designed and typeset by Kamae Design
Original illustrations © Pearson Education Limited 2017, 2023
Illustrated by Fran and David Brylewski, Nigel Dobbyn, Adam Linley, Nadene Naude and Jorge Santillan
at Beehive Illustration; Emily Skinner at Graham-Cameron Illustration; Paul Higgins at Hunter-Higgins Design;
and Kamae Design
Images: The Royal Mint, 1971, 1982, 1990, 1992, 1997, 1998, 2017: 86–96; Bank of England: 87, 89–91, 93, 95
Cover design by Pearson Education Ltd
Front and back cover illustrations by Will Overton at Advocate Art and Nadene Naude at Beehive Illustration

Series Editor: Tony Staneff
Lead author: Josh Lury
Consultant (first edition): Professor Liu Jian and Professor Zhang Dan

The rights of Tony Staneff and Josh Lury to be identified as authors of this work have been asserted by them in
accordance with the Copyright, Designs and Patents Act 1988.

First published 2017
This edition first published 2023

27 26 25 24 23
10 9 8 7 6 5 4 3 2 1

British Library Cataloguing in Publication Data
A catalogue record for this book is available from the British Library

ISBN 978 1 292 41938 1

Printed in the UK by Bell & Bain Ltd, Glasgow

For Power Maths resources go to
www.activelearnprimary.co.uk

Note from the publisher
Pearson has robust editorial processes, including answer and fact checks, to ensure the accuracy of the content in this
publication, and every effort is made to ensure this publication is free of errors. We are, however, only human, and
occasionally errors do occur. Pearson is not liable for any misunderstandings that arise as a result of errors in this
publication, but it is our priority to ensure that the content is accurate. If you spot an error, please do contact us at
resourcescorrections@pearson.com so we can make sure it is corrected.